U.S. WOMEN'S TEAM

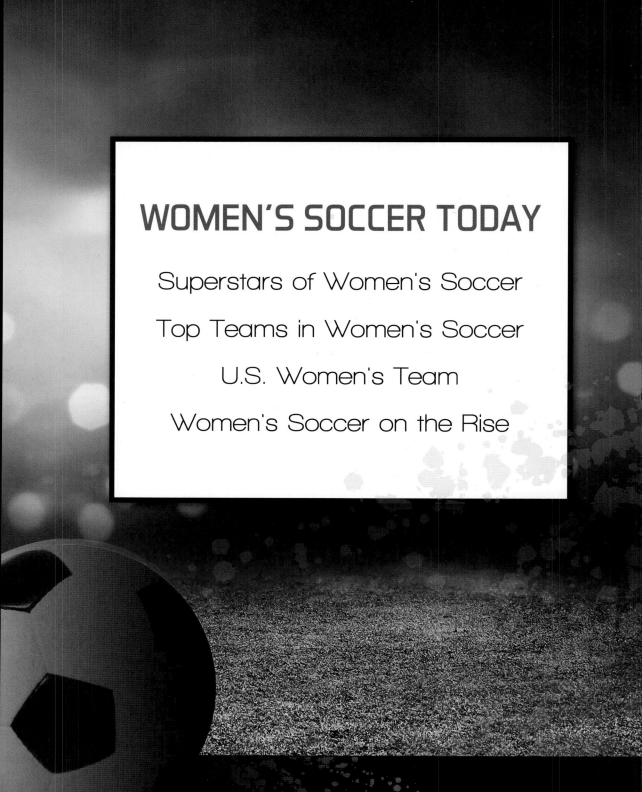

WOMEN'S SOCCER TODAY

Superstars of Women's Soccer

Top Teams in Women's Soccer

U.S. Women's Team

Women's Soccer on the Rise

U.S. WOMEN'S TEAM

ANDREW LUKE

MASON CREST

Mason Crest
450 Parkway Drive, Suite D
Broomall, Pennsylvania 19008
(866) MCP-BOOK (toll free)

First printing
9 8 7 6 5 4 3 2 1

ISBN (hardback) 978-1-4222-4215-5
ISBN (series) 978-1-4222-4212-4
ISBN (ebook) 978-1-4222-7597-9

Library of Congress Cataloging-in-Publication Data on file

Developed and Produced by National Highlights Inc.
Editor: Andrew Luke
Interior and cover design: Annalisa Gumbrecht, Studio Gumbrecht
Production: Michelle Luke

QR CODES AND LINKS TO THIRD-PARTY CONTENT

KEY ICONS TO LOOK FOR:

 WORDS TO UNDERSTAND: These words with their easy-to-understand definitions will increase the reader's understanding of the text while building vocabulary skills.

 SIDEBARS: This boxed material within the main text allows readers to build knowledge, gain insights, explore possibilities, and broaden their perspectives by weaving together additional information to provide realistic and holistic perspectives.

 EDUCATIONAL VIDEOS: Readers can view videos by scanning our QR codes, providing them with additional educational content to supplement the text. Examples include news coverage, moments in history, speeches, iconic sports moments, and much more!

 TEXT-DEPENDENT QUESTIONS: These questions send the reader back to the text for more careful attention to the evidence presented there.

 RESEARCH PROJECTS: Readers are pointed toward areas of further inquiry connected to each chapter. Suggestions are provided for projects that encourage deeper research and analysis.

WORDS TO UNDERSTAND

comprise
to make up or form (something)

indelible
cannot be removed, washed away, or erased

nemesis
a formidable opponent

purging
getting rid of

CHAPTER 1

A History of the U.S. Women's National Team

The United States Women's National Soccer Team (USWNT) may not have the long history of its male counterpart, but what history it does have is far more accomplished. The seventeen women that sewed the USA decal onto their used men's jerseys in 1985 could scarcely have conceived what those accomplishments would be, but that first USWNT was the start of a proud and successful legacy.

THE PIONEERS

The 1985 USWNT was chosen after a group of seventy players was invited to participate in a sports festival soccer tournament in Baton Rouge, Louisiana. The coach, Mike Ryan, was an Irishman who came to America in 1958. Ryan settled in the Seattle area and spent ten years building the University of Washington's men's soccer program.

At the end of the Baton Rouge festival, Ryan selected the players who would comprise the first USWNT squad by calling out their names as they sat on the field after the final match. The most prominent of these first team members was University of Central Florida forward Michelle Akers. The nineteen-year-old and her teammates left for the team's first-ever international tournament just two weeks later after only three days of practice.

SEVEN DAYS IN ITALY

Each team member received a new pair of cleats to go along with her hand-me-down men's jersey, plus ten dollars a day for food in Jesolo, Italy.

The team, captained by University of Washington defender Denise Bender, played four matches over seven days against teams from Denmark (twice), England, and Italy. The Americans lost three of the four matches with one draw, scoring just three goals in total. Two of the goals came from Akers, including the very first goal in USWNT history, in the team's second match against Denmark. Future National Soccer Hall of Fame midfielder Emily Pickering had the other.

The USWNT played its first international match at a tournament in the picturesque town of Jesolo, near Venice, Italy.

Mundialito

Mundialito is Spanish for "little world cup", and over the years the term has been applied to a variety of soccer tournaments. The tournament was first played in 1984, and the first match ever played by the USWNT was at the Mundialito in northern Italy in 1985. At the time, before an actual FIFA-sanctioned event for women existed, this was one of the most important women's tournaments in the world. It was a four-team invitational event held in the town of Jesolo, a coastal town on the Adriatic Sea just outside of Venice. The U.S. team participated three times, with runner-up being its best result, which it earned in 1986. The Jesolo Mundialito was last played in 1988.

This first, quickly assembled USWNT had no success on the field, but its legacy is indelible. However, eight of the players, including Bender, would never play for the USWNT again. Six others played ten or fewer career matches for the national team. Only Akers, Pickering, and her University of North Carolina teammate Lori Henry became fixtures of future teams.

A FRESH START

Mike Ryan was out as coach after that initial tournament, and North Carolina men's and women's head coach Anson Dorrance took over the job in 1986. His NCAA women's team won four of the first five national championships ever awarded in the women's game. Dorrance would also go on to win nine consecutive titles from 1986 to 1994. Dorrance was determined to match the success that his women's team had achieved in the infancy of high-level college competition at the even-newer international level.

Longtime University of North Carolina head coach Anson Dorrance ran the USWNT from 1986 to 1994.

After purging many of the original USWNT players, Dorrance made Pickering the team captain. Then he began adding the women who would become the foundation of future champions. Kristine Lilly, Joy Fawcett, Carin Jennings, and Mia Hamm joined the team in 1987. Brandi Chastain, Carla Overbeck, and Julie Foudy arrived in 1988. All seven women played more than one hundred career matches for the USWNT and, along with Akers, were key pieces of the team for the first-ever Women's World Cup.

1991 FIFA WOMEN'S WORLD CUP

The very first Women's World Cup was not initially known as a World Cup. Officially, it was the FIFA Women's World Championship. FIFA is the sport's international governing body, the Fédération Internationale de Football Association. FIFA had staged what was essentially a world championship trial run in 1988 when it organized an invitational tournament in China for twelve teams. The success of that event led to the go-ahead for the 1991 tournament in Guangdong, China.

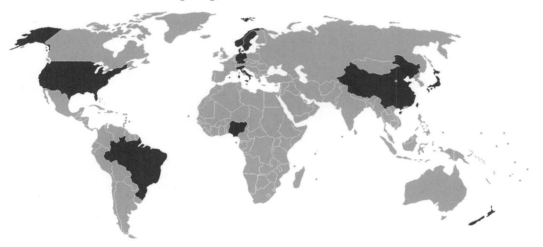

The United States was one of the twelve countries, indicated in blue, to qualify for the first FIFA Women's World Cup.

The Americans qualified easily for the tournament, scoring forty-five goals and giving up none in winning five-straight qualification matches against teams from the Confederation of North, Central America and Caribbean Association Football, known as CONCACAF. This reflects the non-competitive state of women's soccer in CONCACAF at the time. In China, the competition was somewhat stronger, but the Americans played just two matches that were won by fewer than three goals in their undefeated run to the championship victory. Akers had ten goals to lead the tournament in scoring. Dorrance flew in the face of convention with his coaching style, which was vindicated by that 1991 victory. Most teams played a 4-4-2 formation, but the American team played a 3-4-3.

"We were great duelers. We were gritty. We were to some extent irreverent because we didn't worship at the altar of the 4-4-2, and we didn't play the ball around in the back for half an hour to show we could possess it. We were different, and we scared teams because we were different," said Dorrance.

Coach Tony DiCicco added future team captain Christie Rampone to the USWNT in 1997. She went on to play 311 matches at center back.

CHANGING OF THE GUARD

Dorrance continued as coach until 1994. During his eight years in the job, the team piled up a .737 winning percentage. When Dorrance stepped away, the job went to the team's former goalkeeper coach, Tony DiCicco. Under Dorrance, the captaincy passed from Emily Pickering to Lori Henry to Carla Overbeck, who would remain as DiCicco's captain throughout his time as head coach.

DiCicco's first major event as head coach was the 1995 Women's World Cup, which ended in disappointing fashion with a third-place finish. He added two key players during his time running the team. The first was Cindy Parlow, who scored seventy-five goals in a 158-match career that began in 1996. The other was Christie Rampone, a center back who would anchor the USWNT defense for sixteen years starting in 1997.

A STRING OF SUCCESSES

With Parlow added to the core, DiCicco's team earned redemption for falling short at the 1995 World Cup with a superb effort at the 1996 Olympic Games in Atlanta. This was the first Olympic Games to include women's soccer as a medal event. Seven teams qualified for the tournament, including China, Japan, Brazil, Denmark, Germany, Norway, and Sweden. As the host nation, the United States was entered automatically.

Watch the USWNT's run to the first ever women's soccer Olympic gold medal.

The Americans opened the tournament with group stage play, where they won their first two matches before a draw against China in match three. This put them second in the group behind China, as the Chinese had scored more goals. The United States advanced to the semifinals to play the winner of the other group—Norway.

Ann Kristin Aarønes and Linda Medalen, who would be the leading goal scorers in the tournament, led the Norwegians. The match was a tight one, with the Norwegians leading 1–0 late in the second half on the strength of a Medalen goal in the eighteenth minute. A late penalty awarded by the referee gave the Americans the chance to tie, and Akers made no mistake. The match went to extra time tied at 1-1. DiCicco made his only substitution of the match in the ninety-sixth minute, bringing on midfielder Shannon MacMillan. Just four minutes later, Julie Foudy capped a beautiful run with a pass to MacMillan for the golden goal, which is the term for an extra time goal that suddenly ends a match.

The gold-medal match, played in front of nearly eighty thousand people in Athens, GA, gave Team USA another chance to beat China. Neither side had scored in their group stage match. MacMillan changed that trend just nineteen minutes into the match. Lilly made a run down the left side, and her cross found an onrushing Hamm, whose volley was saved by the keeper and then hit the left post and bounced directly to MacMillan for an easy tap in.

China got the equalizer thirteen minutes later, and the two teams started the second half tied 1–1. The Americans kept attacking, however, and were rewarded midway through the half. Fawcett made a run into the penalty area from the right side and slid a pass over to a wide-open Tiffeny Milbrett at the top of the six-yard box for the gold medal winning goal.

Shannon MacMillan led the United States to the gold medal by scoring three goals at the 1996 Olympic Games in Atlanta.

1999 FIFA WOMEN'S WORLD CUP

DiCicco followed-up on Olympic glory at the 1999 Women's World Cup, which was also held in the United States. The USWNT was the favorite, and the players knew the success of the tournament on U.S. soil depended on them doing well. The Americans cruised through the group stage virtually unchallenged, giving up just a single goal in three matches, all victories. Matches were closer in the knockout stage, especially in the final match against nemesis China. The Americans won on penalty kicks, with Brandi Chastain scoring perhaps the most famous goal in women's soccer history for the win.

DiCicco left the team shortly after that World Cup win, having put together a 103–8–8 record in his time as coach. The United States Soccer Federation named April Heinrichs, former player and ex-

USWNT captain from the 1991 World Cup team, as his successor. Her teams struggled to match prior success, and Heinrichs's tenure saw the departure of legends Akers and Hamm, along with Parlow. She did bring on future stars, however, including goalkeeper Hope Solo in 2000, all-time leading scorer Abby Wambach in 2001, and midfielder Heather O'Reilly in 2002.

STRUGGLING FOR RESULTS

The Heinrichs made Foudy and Fawcett cocaptains in 2000, leading up to the team's first major competition on her watch, the 2000 Olympics in Sydney, Australia. The World Cup champions were the favorites to win gold. The group stage produced a similar result to 1996, with two wins plus a draw against China. This time the United States won the group to set up a semifinal against Brazil. Hamm scored the only goal of the match in the sixtieth minute.

Mia Hamm (#9) is shown here playing in her final FIFA Women's World Cup in 2003. She retired the following year after leading the team to the first of three consecutive Olympic gold medals.

In the gold-medal match, the United States faced a strong Norwegian team looking to avenge its loss to Team USA in the 1996 semifinal. Down 2–1 with the last seconds of the match ticking away, Milbrett scored her second goal of the match to send the contest to extra time. The play saw a perfect cross from Hamm to the forehead of Milbrett and into the net as time expired. Twelve minutes into extra time, a cross from Norwegian midfielder Hege Riise bounced off Fawcett's head then off the upper arm of Norwegian forward Dagny Mellgren, who then shot it into the net. No hand ball was called, and the goal stood for the Norwegian win.

Heinrichs was the target of criticism in 2003 during the FIFA Women's World Cup, which was again held in the United States. After another undefeated group stage where it conceded only one goal, Team USA won a tough quarterfinal 1–0 over Norway but was shut out by Germany in the semifinals and settled for third place. In later years, Foudy and Chastain criticized Heinrichs for being inflexible in her approach to that match against the Germans. Milbrett quit the team, citing stifling tactics and unprofessionalism on the part of Heinrichs.

Redemption for Heinrichs came at the 2004 Olympics in Athens, Greece, where the USWNT again conceded just one goal to win its round-robin group. The knockout stage saw successive 2–1

Tiffeny Milbrett (#16) quit the USWNT after the 2003 World Cup, citing unhappiness with coach April Heinrichs' tactics.

wins against Japan, Germany, and Brazil to claim gold. This was the swan song for Hamm, who retired four months later. It was also the last major tournament together for the remaining players from the 1991 World Cup champions—Foudy, Fawcett, Lilly, and Chastain. Lilly took over as captain when Foudy and Fawcett retired in 2004. Athens 2004 was a coming out party for Wambach, who scored four goals in the tournament.

SOMETIMES NUMBERS LIE

The Athens Olympics was also the end for Heinrichs, who stepped down and handed the job to her assistant, Greg Ryan. In his three-year stint, Ryan's teams lost just a single match, with a record of 45–1–9. That reads like a remarkably successful stat line, but few remember Ryan's tenure that way.

Ryan added star midfielder Megan Rapinoe in 2006, and the team was cruising along under Ryan as the 2007 FIFA Women's World Cup approached. He had added superstar midfielder Carli Lloyd out of Rutgers in 2005,

The decision by head coach Greg Ryan to bench starting goalkeeper Hope Solo for disciplinary reasons for the 2007 World Cup semifinals cost the United States the match and Ryan his job.

who along with Wambach provided a lethal 1–2 offensive punch. At the World Cup tournament in China, the Americans went unbeaten to win their group, though perhaps not as easily as expected, scoring just five goals in three matches. They crushed England 3–0 in the quarterfinals, however, so things appeared to be fine until disaster struck in the semifinals against Brazil.

Ryan benched starting goalie Hope Solo, coming off three-straight clean sheets, in favor of veteran Briana Scurry. This was one of a number of decisions that backfired on Ryan, as Brazil handed the Americans their worst loss ever, 4–0. Not one to be shy about expressing her feelings, Solo blasted her coach publicly in an interview with Canadian broadcaster CBC. "It was the wrong decision, and I think that anybody who knows anything about the game knows that. There's no doubt in my mind I would have made those saves and the fact of the matter is, it's not 2004 anymore," Solo said.
Solo was shipped home before the third place match, but a retired Chastain also publicly called for Ryan to be fired, and Foudy publicly questioned his tactics. Ryan was fired in December of that year.

HEAD WOMAN IN CHARGE

In 2008 former Swedish player Pia Sundhage became the second woman to coach the USWNT. She made Rampone the captain, a position which she held until she retired in 2015. Sundhage faced the task of getting the team ready for the Olympic Games in China in just eight months. She was dealt a serious blow when Wambach was lost to a broken leg just three weeks before the Olympics.

The Americans opened the games with a loss to Norway but rebounded to win their group. They then needed an extra-time goal from Natasha Kai to beat Canada in the quarterfinals. In the semifinals, Team USA had no trouble with Japan, before facing Brazil and superstar Marta in the gold-medal match. The match was tight

Head coach Pia Sundhage left after a successful run with the USWNT to take the head job with her native Sweden in 2010.

throughout and went to extra time tied at 0–0. The winning goal for Sundhage and her team came from Lloyd, with a left-footed blast from the top of the penalty area to take the gold.

Sundhage was not as fortunate at the 2011 FIFA Women's World Cup as the Americans came up just short, losing on penalty kicks in the final match to Japan to earn silver medals. The tournament was notable for the performance of the USWNT's youngest player, striker Alex Morgan, who turned twenty-two during the tournament. Coming off the bench, Morgan scored two goals in the knockout round, a precursor to a brilliant career to come.

Sundhage then led the team to a second defense of the Olympic gold medal at the 2012 games in London, where Wambach, Lloyd, and Morgan starred.

A SHORT STINT

Sundhage decided to take the head job coaching for her home country's women's team after her success in 2012. The USWNT job went to Scottish coach Tom Sermanni, whose time with the team was brief. Sermanni's team had an unbeaten record of 13–0–3 in 2013, but a disastrous showing at a tournament in March of 2014 sealed his fate.

The Algarve Cup is an annual twelve-team invitational tournament held in Portugal. Sermanni and the USWNT were the defending champions in 2014 but opened the tournament with a 1–1 draw with Japan and a 1–0 loss to Sweden. With no chance to win the tournament, the tournament, the Americans played poorly in the final group stage match against Denmark. The Danes had yet to score a goal in the tournament, and the Americans allowed them to score five in a 5–3 loss. They finished in seventh place. Sermanni was fired four weeks later.

THE ELLIS ERA

Jill Ellis is an English-born coach who had been on the U.S. Soccer radar for some time. She coached American national youth teams for several years and was an assistant on Sundhage's staff. When Sundhage left, she was named interim coach for four months until Sermanni was hired. When he was fired, the United States Soccer Federation realized that the right person for the job was under its nose all along.

Ellis named Carli Lloyd and Becky Sauerbrunn cocaptains when Rampone retired. Ellis took the USWNT, led on the field by the play of Lloyd and Hope Solo, to its third FIFA Women's World Cup title in 2015. That high was followed quickly by the low point of the 2016 Summer Olympics in Brazil, where the three-time defending gold medalists came in having never finished with less than a silver medal.

Head coach Jill Ellis [right] celebrates the 2015 World Cup victory at a parade for the USWNT in New York, accompanied by Megan Rapinoe (center), Carli Lloyd (left), and New York City mayor Bill de Blasio.

As usual, the Americans went undefeated to win their group. Their reward, however, was a not-so-inviting match up with Sundhage and Sweden in the quarterfinals. The match was a hard fought 0–0 battle until Swedish substitute Stina Blackstenius beat Solo for the first goal of the match in the sixty-first minute. Morgan returned the favor for the Americans sixteen minutes later to equalize and send the match to extra time. Neither team was able to score in extra time, and the match was decided by penalty kicks. After four shooters, it was 3–3 with one shooter remaining for each team. That is when substitute forward Christen Press missed her kick high. Lisa Dahlkvist scored for Sweden, and the Americans were out.

Following the match, Solo called the Swedes cowards for their tactics, earning herself a six-month suspension. The United States Soccer Federation terminated her contract, and she has not played for the USWNT since. She turns thirty-eight years old three weeks after the 2019 FIFA Women's World Cup in France.

The USWNT went 12–3–1 in 2017 and in 2018 qualified easily for the 2019 Women's World Cup. The veteran core of Lloyd, Morgan, Rapinoe, and Sauerbrunn will be joined by a host of up-and-coming young talent as they defend their world title.

TEXT-DEPENDENT QUESTIONS:

1. Who was the first head coach of the USWNT?
2. What was the USWNT's tournament result at the 2000 Summer Olympic Games?
3. Why was Hope Solo's contract terminated in 2016?

RESEARCH PROJECT:

Which was the greatest match in USWNT history? Put together a presentation that includes video from the match and highlights the specific elements that make it stand out above the rest.

30 MILLION
GIRLS AND WOMEN
PLAY FOOTBALL
AROUND THE GLOBE

WORDS TO UNDERSTAND

culminate
to reach the end or the final result of something

dismantled
to destroy (something) in an orderly way

iconic
widely recognized and well-established

retroactively
effective from a particular date in the past

CHAPTER 2

Team USA at the World Cup

The FIFA World Cup is the biggest sporting event in the world today, but that was not the case when it was first held in Uruguay in 1930. While the Women's World Cup is barely a quarter-century old, it is certainly the biggest event in the women's game, and only time will tell what it might eventually become.

THE BEGINNING: 1991

The very first FIFA Women's World Cup was held in China after FIFA held a successful trial tournament there in 1988. The first FIFA World Championship for Women's Football took place in four cities in November of 1991. The name FIFA Women's World Cup was not adopted until the next event in 1995 but was applied **retroactively** to the 1991 event.

Twelve teams in total took part in the event including the host from China, who was granted an automatic entry. The other eleven teams that qualified were Japan, Chinese Taipei, Nigeria, Brazil, Denmark, Germany, Italy, Norway, Sweden, New Zealand, and the United States. A drawing put the teams in three groups of four for a round-robin opening stage.

The United States drew into Group B with Sweden, Brazil, and Japan. Eventually all three of these rival countries would develop into strong women's soccer powers, but in 1991, only Sweden had the talent to challenge the Americans. The USWNT opened the tournament with a hard-fought 3–2 win over the Swedes. After that, both teams easily won their matches against Japan and Brazil to advance to the knockout stage.

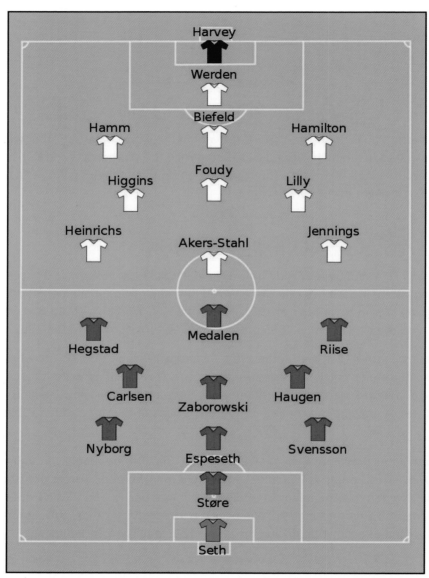

The USWNT starting lineup in the 1991 FIFA Women's World Cup final versus Norway featured Kristine Lilly, Mia Hamm and Julie Foudy, three of the four most capped players in team history.

In the quarterfinals, the Americans drew Chinese Taipei and dismantled them 7–0 behind five goals from Akers, who was the star of the tournament for the United States. The Americans were not challenged in the semifinals either, beating Germany handily 5–2. Akers saved her best effort for the toughest opponent, as Team USA faced Norway in the final.

The match was just twenty minutes old when Akers opened the scoring by jumping high to get her head on a free kick just outside the six-yard box. It was a huge goal for the United States. as Norway had controlled most of the play to start the match. Eight minutes later, Norway equalized on a header by Linda Medalen that caught U.S. goalie Mary Harvey out of position. With just two minutes left, a disastrous mistake by the Norwegian defense caused a dramatic conclusion. A Norwegian defender controlled a long ball into their own half and turned to pass the ball about fifteen yards back to her keeper. She mishit the ball, however, and it trickled just a few yards. Akers, who had been sprinting after the ball, ran past the defender and reached the ball before the goalie, who dove in desperation. Akers dribbled around her and scored into the open net to seal the first-ever world championship in women's soccer.

Akers won the Golden Boot award for most goals scored in the tournament, with ten to her credit. Her partner up front for the United States, Carin Jennings, won the Golden Ball as the tournament's best player. A nineteen-year-old Mia Hamm was the youngest player on the team.

1995 FIFA WOMEN'S WORLD CUP

The 1995 tournament took place in Sweden using the same twelve-team format as the initial 1991 event. China was forced to qualify this time, as it was not the host nation. Canada also qualified as a second team from North America, replacing a team from Asia.

The USWNT found itself in Group C with China, Denmark, and Australia. The Chinese had made great strides in women's soccer in the four years since the first Women's World Cup and gave the heavily favored USWNT a tough match to open the tournament, managing a 3–3 draw. The worst part of the match for the Americans was losing Akers to a knee injury just seven minutes in. Both teams won their remaining matches to advance to the knockout stage. The most notable event in the other group stage matches for the USWNT came in the match against Denmark, when Hamm was forced to play goalkeeper when Briana Scurry was ejected. The United States won 2–0.

In the quarterfinals, the United States had little trouble with the squad from Japan, winning 4–0. The semifinal matchup was a rematch of the 1991 final against a revenge-minded Norwegian team. The match was a defensive struggle, with the only goal coming from Aarønes ten minutes into the first half. The Norwegians went on to win the title by beating Germany.

The Americans salvaged their tournament with another win over China in the third-place match. Lilly and Milbrett each had three goals in the tournament to lead the USWNT. Norway's Hege Riise won the Golden Ball, while Aarønes won the Golden Boot with six goals.

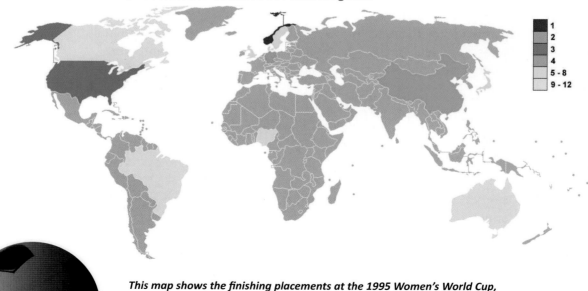

1
2
3
4
5 - 8
9 - 12

This map shows the finishing placements at the 1995 Women's World Cup, including Norway as champions and the United States in third.

1999 FIFA WOMEN'S WORLD CUP

The 1999 event was historic for the United States for a number of reasons. One reason was that the United States was the host nation for the first time. Matches were held across the country from Southern California to New England. Also, the field expanded from twelve to sixteen teams, with one additional team qualifying from Africa, Asia, Europe, and North America. This meant an additional group of four, with the top two teams in each of the four groups advancing to the knockout stage.

The tournament set new records for attendance, media coverage, and television viewership for women's soccer. The final alone had more than ninety thousand spectators in attendance, a record at the time for a women's event in any sport.

Now a successful soccer commentator, Brandi Chastain scored the penalty kick that won the 1999 FIFA Women's World Cup for the United States, one of the most iconic moments in women's sports.

On the field, the Americans dominated Group A, outscoring Nigeria, North Korea, and Denmark. In the quarterfinals, the United States met a very capable German side and had to come from behind to win 3–2. The Americans played well in the semifinals, shutting out Brazil 2–0 to set up a final against China.

The final was a defensive battle that culminated in epic fashion for the USWNT. Neither team was able to score in regulation time, and the tight defensive play continued through extra time to force a penalty kick shoot-out with the score tied 0–0.

Each team made its first two kicks, with Overbeck and Fawcett scoring for the Americans. On China's third kick, however, Scurry guessed correctly by diving to her left and got her hand on the

27

shot by Liu Ying to make the save. Lilly made her kick, as did the next Chinese shooter, followed by Hamm and the fifth Chinese shooter, both of whom also converted.

With the shoot-out tied at 4–4, only veteran defender Brandi Chastain remained to shoot. If she scored, the United States would be champions of the world. With no hesitation, she drove a left-footed shot high into the right side of the net, well beyond the reach of the leaping keeper. Chastain's reaction to scoring the tournament-winning goal would prove to be one of the most iconic in American sports. As her teammates rushed from midfield to celebrate with her, Chastain pulled her jersey over her head and dropped to her knees, flexing her chiseled body in sheer triumph. She stood as her teammates arrived to embrace her, but the photo of Chastain kneeling in celebration, jersey clutched in her right fist and joy exploding across her face became one of the best-known images in sports. The image appeared on the covers of *Sports Illustrated, Newsweek,* and *Time* magazines.

Check out the highlights of the American triumph at the 1999 Women's World Cup.

Chastain was one of five Americans named to the tournament all-star team along with Overbeck, Hamm, Akers, and Scurry. Sissi of Brazil scored seven goals to lead the tournament and claim the Golden Boot, while Sun Wen of China won the Golden Ball as best player. It was the first time the host country had won the championship.

2003 FIFA WOMEN'S WORLD CUP

The 2003 tournament was due to take place in China. However, when the country was stricken with an outbreak of the deadly and highly-contagious disease known as SARS, FIFA made the decision to move the event to the United States once again.

Due to an outbreak of the deadly SARS virus in Asia, the 2003 FIFA Women's World Cup was moved from China to the United States.

Six U.S. cities played host to the sixteen teams, which included two each from Africa, South America, and North America; one from Oceania; and four each from Europe and Asia, including China, which retained host nation status.

The United States drew into Group A with Sweden, North Korea, and Nigeria and went untested in winning the group by outscoring opponents 11–1. Winning the group sent the USWNT to a quarterfinal matchup with rival Norway, where an early Wambach goal held up for the 1–0 win. In the semifinals, the United Stated faced a strong German squad led by the outstanding goalkeeper Silke Rottenberg. The Americans could not get a shot past Rottenberg, who made several key saves in support of a first-half goal by Kerstin Garefrekes. The Germans scored two late goals in added time to win 3–0, disappointing more than twenty-seven thousand fans in Portland, OR.

Team USA did win the third-place match against Canada behind goals from Kristine Lilly, Tiffeny Milbrett, and Shannon Boxx, while Germany went on to win the tournament against Sweden. Fawcett and Boxx were named to the tournament all-star team, and Golden Boot winner Birgit Prinz of Germany also won the Golden Ball.

2007 FIFA WOMEN'S WORLD CUP

With the SARS epidemic in the past, China was permitted to host the 2007 FIFA Women's World Cup. The sixteen-team format remained in place, and five venues were used across the country to host the event.

This time, the United States was in Group B, coincidentally matched against North Korea, Sweden, and Nigeria for the second straight World Cup. The opponents were the same, but this version of the USWNT struggled to score goals, managing to win the group while scoring just five goals in three matches. Solo kept the team alive by posting two clean-sheet wins after allowing two goals in an opening-match draw with North Korea.

Abby Wambach scored a team-leading six goals for the USWNT at the 2007 FIFA Women's World Cup.

In the quarterfinals against England, Solo was strong again stifling English star Kelly Smith and her team. Wambach, Boxx, and Lilly scored to give the United States a 3–0 win. That strong offensive showing by Team USA was followed by one of the worst performances in team history.

Going into the semifinals against Brazil, Solo had allowed just two goals in four matches, including three consecutive clean sheets. Inexplicably, head coach Greg Ryan opted to bench Solo in favor of Scurry, who, at age thirty-six, was the veteran backup keeper. At the time, Ryan said he needed a more "reaction-save" goalie, but no one that followed the sport believed that. He later revealed that he benched Solo because she missed the team dinner and broke curfew the night before the match against England. It was a costly decision. In the match, the Americans could not shake off an early own goal by midfielder Leslie Osborne, and Brazilian superstar Marta scored twice as Team USA fell 4–0.

Solo openly criticized Scurry's play and Ryan's decision after the match and was sent home before the third-place match against Norway. In that match, the team rallied around Scurry and beat the Norwegians 4–1 for a second consecutive third-place finish. The damage was done, however, and the U.S. Soccer Federation fired Ryan following the tournament. The loss to Brazil, which was beaten by Germany in the final, was the only loss to the Brazillian team, which Ryan suffered in his tenure as head coach.

2011 FIFA WOMEN'S WORLD CUP

The women's soccer world converged on Germany for the 2011 FIFA Women's World Cup, a tournament that again used the sixteen-team format. Under head coach Pia Sundhage, however, the USWNT struggled during qualification, needing to win a playoff against Italy to make the field.

Team USA drew into Group C with Sweden, North Korea, and Colombia. The Americans started well, as Solo posted clean sheets in the 2–0 win over North Korea in the opener and a 3–0 win over Colombia in match number two. Match three against unbeaten Sweden would determine the winner of the group.

Swedish captain, defender Nilla Fischer, scored the winning goal against the USWNT during the group stage of the 2011 FIFA Women's World Cup.

The Swedes had also yet to concede a goal going into the early tournament showdown with Team USA. The Swedes struck first as the referee called a penalty against the United States, and Solo was finally beaten on the ensuing penalty kick. Sweden struck again before the half was over, as Nilla Fischer scored five minutes before the half ended. The Americans finally got one back on a goal from Wambach in the sixty-seventh minute. That proved to be too little too late, however, as the Americans could not find the equalizer and lost 2–1 to finish second in the group.

The second-place finish meant a tough quarterfinal matchup against Marta and Brazil—a rematch of the semifinals from 2007. The Americans got the first break early on, as a Brazilian defender knocked a Boxx cross into her own goal. The 1–0 lead stood for sixty-six minutes, when United States center back Rachel Buehler pulled down a hard-charging Marta in the six-yard box. Not only did the referee award a penalty, but she showed Buehler a red card, ejecting her from the match. Brazilian midfielder Cristiane took the penalty kick, but it was saved by Solo. On a controversial call, the referee disqualified the kick, ruling that Rampone had entered the penalty area before the kick. So the penalty was retaken, this time with Marta as the shooter, and she buried it to tie the match at 1–1. The match went to extra time.

Just two minutes into extra time Marta struck again, looping a shot over Solo's head from in close for the 2–1 lead. Playing with just ten women, the Americans struggled to play catchup and still trailed as the clock ticked into added time in the extra period. That is when Rapinoe and Wambach combined for one of the greatest goals in USWNT history.

From thirty yards out all the way over near the left-side touch line, Rapinoe delivered a booming left-footed cross to the top of the six-yard box. Arriving at the same time as the ball was Wambach, who headed the ball past the disbelieving goalkeeper to tie the match and send it to penalty kicks. In the shoot-out, the first four shooters,

Finishing second in its group to Sweden meant the USWNT had to face a tough Brazil team led by Marta to open the knockout stage.

Cristiane and Marta for Brazil and Boxx and Lloyd for the United States, all made their kicks. The third Brazilian shooter was Daiane Rodrigues, who had scored on her own goal to begin the match. She aimed her shot to the left side, which is exactly what Solo guessed she would do. The American keeper got her right hand on the ball to deflect it away. The final three U.S. shooters all made their kicks to complete the improbable comeback.

In the semifinals against France, a Wambach goal in the seventy-ninth minute broke a 1–1 tie and propelled the USWNT to a 3–1 win and a matchup with Japan in the final. The final was an emotional roller coaster for the United States. A sixty-ninth minute goal by Alex Morgan to put the United States ahead 1–0 looked like it might hold up, but Japan scored the equalizer with nine minutes left to send the match to extra time. In extra time, the Americans again looked like they might win after Wambach's goal in the 104th minute. Then Japanese star Homare Sawa scored with just three minutes remaining to force a shoot-out. Unlike the shoot-out against Brazil, this one was a disaster for the United States. Japanese keeper Ayumi Kaihori stopped Boxx on a brilliant diving save. Then Lloyd sailed her kick over the crossbar. When Kaihori guessed right to stop Tobin Heath, the U.S. team's chances evaporated. They could not recover from having the first three shooters fail, and Japan won the shoot-out and the title.

Japanese goalkeeper Ayumi Kaihori made two saves in the final match penalty kick shoot-out to give Japan the 2011 FIFA Women's World Cup title over the United States.

Sawa won the Golden Ball and the Golden Boot with five goals. Solo, Boxx, Wambach, and midfielder Lauren Cheney of the United States were all named to the tournament all-star team.

2015 FIFA WOMEN'S WORLD CUP

The Americans traveled to Canada in 2015 looking for redemption. That year included a fresh look for the event, which had expanded to include twenty-four teams: five from Asia, three from Africa, three from North and Central America, three from South America, one from Oceania, and eight from Europe plus the host nation.

There were now six groups of four teams, with group winners and runners-up advancing along with the four best third-place teams. The second-ranked Americans drew into a difficult Group D with Australia, Sweden (both ranked in the top ten), and Nigeria. As expected, the Americans won the group allowing just one goal and not losing a match. In the sixteen-group knockout stage, the Americans played twenty-eighth-ranked Colombia, which had finished third in its group. Team USA won easily 2–0.

In 2015, FIFA expanded the Women's World Cup field to twenty-four teams, with the associated countries represented in blue on this map.

The difficult tests began in the next round, starting with old nemesis China. A second-half goal by Lloyd held up for a 1–0 win. The semifinal matchup came against the number-one team in the world in the FIFA rankings—Germany. It was a tight match between the world's top-ranked teams that turned on penalty kicks. U.S. defender Julie Johnston pulled down German forward Alexandra Popp in the penalty area in the fifty-ninth minute. The ensuing penalty kick was taken by Célia Šašić, who pushed her shot wide of the left post. Ten minutes later, Annike Krahn bowled over Alex Morgan at the top of the area. Lloyd took the penalty kick and scored cleanly. Kelley O'Hara added a late goal for the 2–0 U.S. win.

Must See TV

The 2015 FIFA Women's World Cup was not just a victory for the USWNT, but it was also a victory for the sport of women's soccer. The Americans beat Japan in the final and beat every other soccer match in U.S. history, men's or women's, in the television ratings. More than twenty-five million viewers tuned in to watch, 77 percent more than watched the 2011 final in which the USWNT also played Japan.

A women's match also held the previous record for U.S. soccer viewership. Eighteen million people watched the USWNT win the 1999 World Cup on Brandi Chastain's dramatic penalty kick.

The chance at redemption came in the final, as the United States was once again battling Japan for the title. With this match, the Americans would decisively erase the humiliation of the 2011 penalty kick shoot-out. In front of fifty-three thousand mostly American fans in Vancouver, the Americans ended the match almost as soon as it began. Team captain Carli Lloyd, who

For the second consecutive Women's World Cup, the United States met Japan in the final match.

had missed the goal entirely on her shoot-out attempt in 2011, scored a hat trick in the first sixteen minutes, including two goals in the first five minutes. Lauren Holiday also scored, and a third of the way into the half it was already 4–0. Japan could not muster a comeback of that magnitude, and the Americans cruised to their third World Cup victory, winning 5–2.

Lloyd was named Player of the Match and also won the Golden Ball as player of the tournament. Lloyd and Šašić were coleaders with six goals scored each. Along with Lloyd, other USWNT members named to the tournament all-star team included Solo, Johnston, Rapinoe, and defender Meghan Klingenberg.

Jill Ellis's squad followed up the 2015 World Cup win with an uninspired performance at the 2016 Olympics, so the 2019 World Cup in France will be the next opportunity for the USWNT to show it is still a force to be reckoned with on the world stage.

Members of the USWNT celebrate their 2015 FIFA Women's World Cup victory during a parade in New York City.

TEXT-DEPENDENT QUESTIONS:

1. Which country hosted the first FIFA Women's World Cup in 1991?
2. Why was the 2007 FIFA Women's World cup held in the United States?
3. Who scored a hat trick in the 2015 FIFA Women's World Cup final?

RESEARCH PROJECT:

Team USA is clearly the most successful team in Women's World Cup history, but which team is next best? Put together a chart that compares and contrasts the successes of teams from Germany, Norway, Japan, and Sweden. Which of the four do you think has been the next-best team? Be sure to provide support for your opinion.

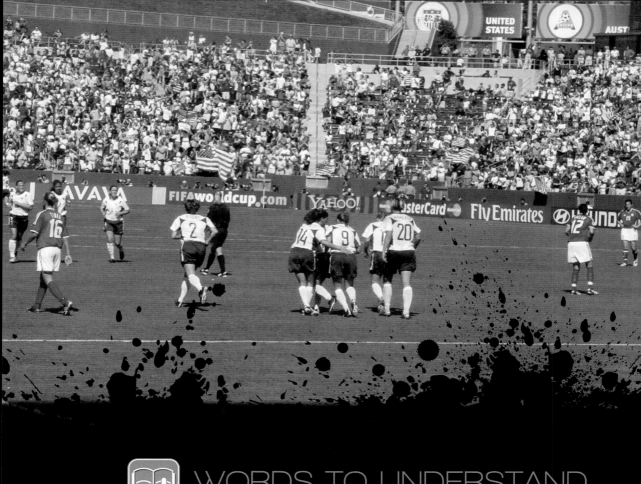

WORDS TO UNDERSTAND

chronic traumatic encephalopathy (CTE)
a progressive neurological disease that is found
in athletes (such as boxers, wrestlers, or football
players) that have experienced repetitive mild injury
to the brain

exuberant
joyously unrestrained and enthusiastic

honed
to make more acute, intense, or effective

CHAPTER 3

Past Stars of Team USA

From the early days of high-level international women's soccer, the United States has had consistently good teams. That makes it no surprise that the history of Team USA is filled with some of the best players to ever play the women's game.

MIA HAMM

When Mia Hamm burst onto the national scene in 1987 as a fifteen-year-old phenom she quickly became the face of American soccer—a role in which she never seemed quite comfortable. At the 1991 Women's World Cup, Hamm was still the youngest player on the team. To this day, she remains the youngest player ever to play for the USWNT.

Hamm's talent was unmatched at the time. She played for USWNT coach Anson Dorrance at North Carolina, where her teams lost one match in four seasons. The Atlantic Coast Conference named Hamm and fellow Tar Heel, basketball legend Michael Jordan, the greatest athletes in the ACC's first fifty years.

From her forward position, she scored a lot of goals and set up even more for Team USA. No American player, male or

Mia Hamm is the all-time leading scorer in USWNT history and is considered by most to be the best female soccer player ever.

female, has assisted on more goals than Hamm's 144 or scored more career points than her total of 302. Only Abby Wambach scored more goals.

MIA HAMM

U.S. WOMEN'S NATIONAL TEAM

2X
FIFA Women's
World Player
of the Year
(2001,2002)

276 CAPS

145
ASSISTS

158
GOALS
8 in the
World Cup,
5 in the Olympics

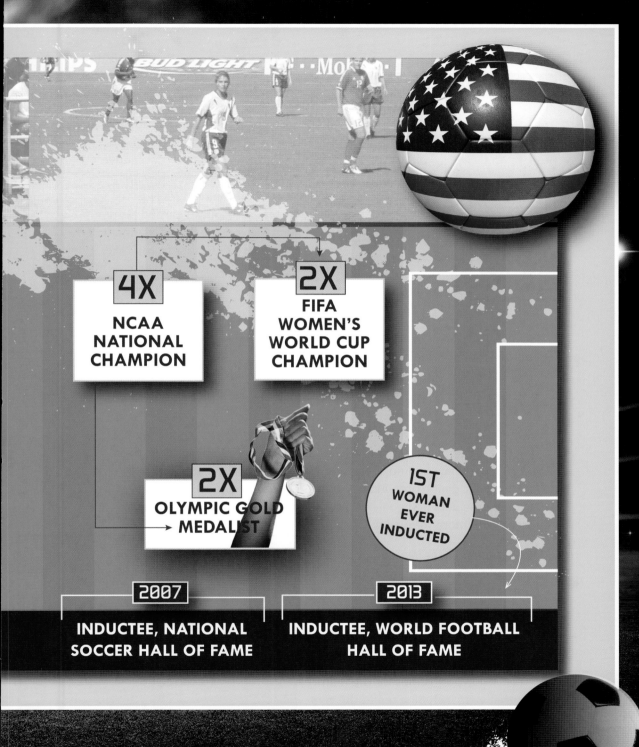

4X

NCAA NATIONAL CHAMPION

2X

FIFA WOMEN'S WORLD CUP CHAMPION

2X

OLYMPIC GOLD MEDALIST

1ST WOMAN EVER INDUCTED

2007

INDUCTEE, NATIONAL SOCCER HALL OF FAME

2013

INDUCTEE, WORLD FOOTBALL HALL OF FAME

No one has had an impact on soccer in America like Mia Hamm. Learn a little about how she did it here.

In the 1990s, Hamm was the face of not just soccer but of female sports in America. She was never team captain but led by the example of her play on the field, for which she won five consecutive U.S. Female Player of the Year awards. Her demeanor off the field was just as admirable. These qualities earned Hamm an excellent living through endorsement deals with giants like Gatorade and Nike. Hamm retired in 2004 after 276 caps as a two-time World Cup champion, a two-time Olympic gold medalist, and winner of the first two Best FIFA Women's Player awards ever in 2001 and 2002. She is the only woman in the World Football Hall of Fame.

MICHELLE AKERS

Michelle Akers was one of the first seventeen players chosen for Team USA in 1985 and one of the few to be kept on when Dorrance took over in 1986. Dorrance had no choice, as she was by far the team's best player and a prolific goal scorer. Akers scored 107 goals in just 155 matches, including the very first goal in USWNT history. Only Wambach has ever scored with more frequency.

Akers grew up near Seattle but played college soccer at the University of Central Florida, where she was a four-time All American. In 1991 Hamm was still just nineteen, and Akers was the engine that drove Team USA. She scored a whopping thirty-nine goals in just twenty-six games for the team that year, including ten at the very

Michelle Akers played college soccer at the University of Central Florida in Orlando.

first FIFA Women's World Cup. The United States took home the trophy, and Akers won the Golden Boot as top goal scorer.

Akers retired in 2000 as a three-time U.S Female Player of the Year award winner and went into the National Soccer Hall of Fame in 2002. In 2004, a FIFA committee headed by the great Pelé named Hamm and Akers as two of the 125 greatest living soccer players. They were the only women to make the list.

ABBY WAMBACH

Scoring goals was what Abby Wambach loved, what she did, and what she was good at. Wambach grew up near Rochester, NY, with six brothers and sisters before making the bold decision to join the new soccer program at the University of Florida beginning with the 1998 season. After leading the Gators to four Southeastern Conference titles and a national title, Wambach earned a shot at making the USWNT in 2001, and the rest is history.

Wambach went on to score 184 goals in her international career, which is .72 per game over 256 matches, a Team USA record. At 5 feet 11 inches (1.8 meters) tall she towered over most defenders and had a huge advantage on high balls. Wambach helped

No player in USWNT history has scored more goals than Abby Wambach's 184.

lead the USWNT to three consecutive Olympic gold medals from 2004 to 2012 and was named the Best FIFA Women's Player in the world in 2011. She retired in 2015 after the United States won the 2015 Women's World Cup, during which she came off the bench as a substitute in most matches. The United States may never see another goal scorer like this six-time U.S. Female Player of the Year award winner.

KRISTINE LILLY

No one in USWNT history played more matches than Connecticut's Kristine Lilly. Only Hamm and Wambach have more goals than the versatile, durable, and tiny (5 feet 4 inches, 1.63 meters) forward/midfielder. Only Hamm has more assists. In 354 matches from 1987 to 2010, Lilly won two Women's World Cups and three Olympic gold medals. She was team captain from 2004 to 2008.

Lilly was also a product of the Dorrance soccer factory at UNC, where she won four-straight NCAA championships and the Hermann Trophy as the best player in the country. She went on to play in a women's record five World Cups and became the oldest woman ever to score at a World Cup with a goal at the 2007 event—she was thirty-six years old. The year before, Lilly was runner-up for the Best FIFA Women's Player award. She won two U.S. Female Player of the Year awards in her career. Lilly was inducted to the National Soccer Hall of Fame in 2015.

All-time USWNT caps leader Kristine Lilly (holding child) poses with her USWNT teammates Abby Wambach (left), Shannon Boxx, and Christie Rampone [right] while playing for the Women's Professional Soccer All-Stars in 2009.

JOY FAWCETT

Joy Fawcett is the best defender ever to play for the USWNT. She represented her country 241 times from 1987 to 2004, the same career span as Hamm. Fawcett captained the team in the last five seasons of her career, which included two World Cup championships and two Olympic gold medals.

A Southern California native, Fawcett honed her defensive skills at the University of California at Berkeley, where she was a three-time All-American. She went on to be the anchor of the USWNT defense for eighteen years, rarely missing a single minute, except when taking time off along the way to have three children. During her playing career, Fawcett also served five seasons as the head coach of the women's soccer program at UCLA.

The All-Time Best

Many people have different opinions about who the most talented women ever to wear the Team USA colors on the pitch were. U.S. Soccer gave its opinion in 2013 when it named its squad of the All-Time Best XI players in USWNT history. A fifty-six-member committee made the selections. Only two of the players, Mia Hamm and Joy Fawcett, were named on all fifty-six ballots. The players were selected using a 4-3-3 formation.

GK – Briana Scurry
D – Joy Fawcett
D – Carla Overbeck
D – Christie Rampone
D – Brandi Chastain
MF – Michelle Akers

MF – Kristine Lilly
MF – Julie Foudy
F – Mia Hamm
F – Abby Wambach
F – Alex Morgan

HOPE SOLO

The statistical record of Washington native Hope Solo on the international stage is staggering. The fiery, outspoken, 5 feet 9 inch (1.75 meters) goalkeeper registered 102 clean sheets in her 202 matches for the USWNT. No other goalie of either sex has one hundred international clean sheets. She once went fifty-five straight matches without a loss. Solo also has more wins than any other keeper in USWNT history.

Solo played college soccer in her home state at the University of Washington, where she was PAC-10 Player of the Year as a sophomore, an award never before given to a goaltender. Also during her sophomore season, Solo made her USWNT debut in April of 2000. She was an alternate on the gold-medal-winning team at the 2004 Olympics in Athens and took over as the starter when Greg Ryan was promoted to head coach in 2005.

Solo and Ryan clashed after a stunning loss at the 2007 Women's World Cup, when she openly criticized his decision to bench her for missing curfew, resulting in her dismissal from the USWNT. Ryan was subsequently fired, and she was reinstated as the starter when Pia Sundhage took over.

Solo then went on a historic run establishing herself as the best goalkeeper in the world. With Solo in the net, the USWNT

No goalkeeper in USWNT history won more matches than two-time World Cup Golden Glove winner Hope Solo.

won two straight Olympic gold medals and was runner-up in the 2011 World Cup before winning the 2015 event. Solo's USWNT career ended in controversy after the 2016 Olympic game's quarterfinal loss to Sweden. Solo called her opponents "a bunch of cowards" following the defeat. Her contract was terminated in August of 2016, effectively ending her outstanding international career. Solo is still the only goalkeeper ever to be named U.S. Female Player of the Year (2009).

When her career ended in 2016, Solo (seen here speaking at the Web Summit event in Portugal in 2017) was one of just ten players with more than 200 USWNT caps.

TIFFENY MILBRETT

Portland native Tiffeny Milbrett stands just 5 feet 2 inches (1.57 meters) tall, but the speedy forward could find the net with the best of them. Milbrett played college soccer at the University of Portland, earning a spot on the USWNT during her sophomore season in 1991. In 206 matches she scored exactly one hundred times, with many of those goals assisted by her longtime forward partner Mia Hamm. Although she had dazzling one-on-one ball skills, Milbrett often returned the favor for Hamm. Only Hamm, Lilly, and Wambach have more career assists than Milbrett.

The 1995 Women's World Cup was Milbrett's coming-out party, when she scored three goals to colead the team in scoring. Milbrett had two United States Female Player of the Year awards, two World Cup titles, and two Olympic gold medals when she retired in 2005.

JULIE FOUDY

Julie Foudy was the midfield anchor on those great USWNT squads of the 1990s. She played 274 matches from 1988 to 2004 (five of those seasons as team cocaptain), collecting forty-five goals and fifty-five assists along the way. The Southern California native starred at Stanford while also playing for the USWNT. During the summer after her sophomore season with the Cardinal, Foudy started for coach Anson Dorrance at the very first Women's World Cup in China, feeding the ball to Michelle Akers and Carin Jennings as the Americans won the tournament.

Following a third-place finish in 1995, Foudy cemented her USWNT legacy by winning the 1999 Women's World Cup. Along with Hamm, Fawcett, and Chastain, she was part of the core group that became known as the "99ers," in reference to that 1999 victory. The players retired as a group following a ten-game victory tour after adding the 2004 Olympic gold medal to their resumes. In 2007 Foudy went into the Hall of Fame in the same class as her longtime teammate Hamm. She continues to work as a strong advocate for equal treatment for the women's teams in the national program, as she did throughout her distinguished career.

Julie Foudy poses with her kids prior to the 2015 ESPY awards in Los Angeles, where she was a presenter.

CHRISTIE RAMPONE

From 1997 to 2015, Christie Rampone roamed the back line for the USWNT, collecting 311 caps. When she took over in 2008, Sundhage gave Rampone the captaincy. Rampone led the team to two gold medals and a World Cup in seven seasons with the armband. She was, of course, also part of the 1999 World Cup champions, although she was not a starter in her early years on the team. In 2015, at the age of forty, she became the oldest player to play in a Women's World Cup.

Rampone is a New Jersey native who played college soccer in her home state at Monmouth University, where she starred as a forward. Rampone set school records for goals, assists, and points in her senior season. She switched to defense while trying to make the USWNT roster the next year, a move that changed the course of her stellar career.

CARLA OVERBECK

Overshadowed somewhat by Fawcett, but not to be discounted, was her partner on defense, Carla Overbeck. USWNT head coach Dorrance knew her well at the beginning of her international career because she played four undefeated seasons for him at UNC from 1986 to 1989. She debuted for Dorrance's Team USA in 1988. The Dallas-area native helped the USWNT win the inaugural World Cup in 1991, the 1996 Olympic gold medal, and the 1999 World Cup.

Christie Rampone (left) challenges teammate Amy LePeilbet during practice at the 2011 FIFA Women's World Cup in Germany.

Dorrance named Overbeck captain of the national team in 1993, a job she held through two coaching changes. She retired in 2000 with 170 career caps and went into the National Soccer Hall of Fame in 2006.

BRIANA SCURRY

Minneapolis born Briana Scurry was the goalkeeper of record for the USWNT during its heyday in the 1990s. After her senior season at the University of Massachusetts ended with a loss to Dorrance, Hamm, and UNC in the 1993 national semifinal, Dorrance invited

her to try out for the national team. Scurry became the full-time starter in 1994, backstopping the United States to wins at the 1996 and 2004 Olympics and the 1999 World Cup.

Overall, Scurry played in four Women's World Cups—no goalkeeper has played in more. Her 173 caps included seventy-one clean sheets. Scurry retired from international play in 2008.

BRANDI CHASTAIN

Brandi Chastain grew up playing the game as a forward in San Jose, CA, and at Santa Clara University. She made the jump to the national team as a midfielder in 1988, but it was the switch to defender in 1996 by coach Tony DiCicco that brought out the best in her game. Chastain is probably the second-most famous American soccer player behind Hamm, all due to one unforgettable celebration in 1999.

After scoring the tournament-winning penalty kick at the 1999 FIFA Women's World Cup, Brandi Chastain burst into the most famous celebration in all of women's sports.

Chastain, of course, scored the Women's World Cup winning penalty kick in 1999 and her iconic, **exuberant**, shirtless celebration is one of the top moments in sports. Chastain was more than just that one moment as a player, however. She played 192 matches for her country and brought a necessary element to the back line anchored by Fawcett and Overbeck.

Chastain went on to be one of the most outspoken voices in the sport after retiring in 2004. She is a popular commentator, female athlete advocate, and spokesperson. Chastain announced in 2016 that she would donate her brain to the study of **chronic traumatic encephalopathy (CTE)**. She was elected to the National Soccer Hall of Fame the same year.

The past stars of Team USA left a tremendous legacy and radically changed the popularity of the sport for women in America. It will be a hard act to follow, but U.S. Soccer is relying on the young girls that grew up being inspired by the sport's pioneers to take it to the next level.

Text-Dependent Questions:

1. How old was Mia Hamm when she first played for the USWNT?

2. How many career international clean sheets did Hope Solo keep?

3. Where is Christie Rampone from?

Research Project:

Who would you choose as the greatest player in USWNT history? Name your favorite, and write a two-page profile that leaves no doubt that you made the correct choice.

 # WORDS TO UNDERSTAND

anterior cruciate ligament (ACL)
a tough, fibrous band of tissue in each knee that attaches the front of the tibia to the back of the femur and functions to prevent hyperextension of the knee; subject to injury, especially by tearing

clairvoyant
able to see beyond the range of ordinary perception

stalwart
solid, dependable, and courageous

star turn
a heralded or impressive performance that raises the profile of the person that gives it

CHAPTER 4

American Stars of World Cup 2019

The focus of soccer fans around the world will be on France in 2019 for the Women's World Cup. The United States will be looking to repeat as champions against a host of tough contenders from the likes of England, Germany, and Canada. It will be up to the new generation of American stars and a few wily veterans to defend the American crown.

CARLI LLOYD

As the veteran cocaptain of the USWNT, Carli Lloyd is approaching legendary status. She led the team to Women's World Cup glory in 2015 in dramatic fashion when she scored three goals in sixteen minutes in the final match against Japan. Lloyd was named Player of the Match for the final and for all four of the USWNT knockout-stage matches. Her performance in that championship was a Golden Ball–winning effort. That year and the following year, 2016, Lloyd was named the Best FIFA Women's Player. She is only the fourth woman to win the award more than once and just the third American ever to win it, joining Hamm (who also won consecutive awards) and Wambach. In 2017, Lloyd was runner-up for the FIFA award to Dutch midfielder Lieke Martens. Lloyd also has U.S. Female Player of the Year awards for 2008 and 2015.

Lloyd grew up in southern New Jersey and displayed the skills to be a dominant midfielder early on. After a brilliant high school career, Lloyd stayed close to home for college. She attended Rutgers University, where she led the team in scoring and was Big East Rookie of the Year. When she graduated college in 2004 she also graduated on the national level, moving from the youth team to the senior team. She made her first USWNT appearance in 2005.

In more than 250 career USWNT matches, Lloyd has helped win two Olympic gold medals and the 2015 Women's World Cup. She has piled up more than one hundred goals along the way and assisted on more than fifty others. She started her career with one goal in her first twenty-four matches, but coach Greg Ryan saw her hard work and determination and banked on that helping her skill finally come through. Lloyd certainly rewarded his patience. Now Lloyd is one of the best players in the world and one of the very best American players of all time.

Carli Lloyd and Mia Hamm are the only Americans ever to win consecutive awards for Best FIFA Women's Player.

France 2019 will be Lloyd's fourth Women's World Cup, and her teams have never finished worse than third. With Lloyd controlling things in the middle of the field, anything less than another appearance in the final match in 2019 would be a disappointment.

Milestone Moment

On April 8, 2018, the USWNT played the second of back-to-back friendly matches against neighboring Mexico. It was not much of a match as matches go—an easy 6–2 win for the United States as the Americans gave the fans in Houston plenty to cheer about.

The match was noteworthy, however, for more than head coach Jill Ellis' experimentation with the lineup. One of the six U.S. goals was scored by cocaptain Carli Lloyd, the one hundredth goal of the star midfielder's career. It was a huge personal accomplishment for the two-time Olympic goal medalist and World Cup champion in her 252nd USWNT match. Only five other players in the program's history have managed one hundred goals: Abby Wambach, Mia Hamm, Kristine Lilly, Michelle Akers, and Tiffeny Milbrett.

Lloyd gets a hug from teammate Alex Morgan as they celebrate a goal against Japan at the 2012 Summer Olympic Games in London.

ALEX MORGAN

Southern California native Alex Morgan is really good at scoring goals. It took her less than 140 matches to move into seventh on the all-time USWNT goal-scoring list. Only Akers and Wambach have scored with more frequency in Team USA history. Morgan has been scoring goals since her years at Diamond Bar High School and playing club soccer.

Morgan went to college at UC Berkeley, where she was an instant star at striker for the Golden Bears. She led the team in scoring as a freshman, as she would continue to do in all four years of her college career. In the spring of her senior year, Morgan played her first match for the USWNT. She had played a couple of prior seasons with the national youth team. Throughout 2010 Sundhage increased her playing time, ultimately deciding to include Morgan on the roster for the 2011 FIFA Women's World Cup in Germany. Sundhage would

Despite being just twenty-four years old at the time, Alex Morgan was named one of the three best forwards in USWNT history in 2013.

have been hard-pressed to keep Morgan off the team after she scored the winning goal in stoppage time against Italy to win a playoff match to qualify for the tournament.

Morgan was the youngest player on that team, turning twenty-two in the first week of the tournament. She played in four of the six

Alex Morgan talks about the epic Olympic semifinal match against Canada in 2012.

USWNT matches, all as a substitute, scoring her first World Cup goal in the final match loss to Japan. Morgan was notable throughout the tournament for the same quality that always got her noticed growing up—her speed. Morgan can put enormous pressure on defenders with her pace, but her other skills are plentiful as well.

It was Morgan's jumping ability that helped her set a FIFA record in 2012 at the Olympic Games in Brazil. The United States had advanced to the semifinals against Canada, and the back-and-forth match stretched late into extra time. It was three minutes into stoppage time, with the final whistle imminent in a 3–3 match, when Morgan leapt above a Canadian defender to head in a cross for the win.

It was the latest goal ever in a FIFA match, scored in the 123rd minute. The Americans went on to win gold. Morgan finished 2012 with a whopping twenty-eight goals and ended up third in the FIFA Women's World Player of the Year voting. She easily won the U.S. Female Player of the Year award that season.

Morgan (left) celebrates with several USWNT teammates at a parade to celebrate Team USA's victory at the 2015 FIFA Women's World Cup.

Now a veteran of the team, Morgan is the face of U.S. Soccer. She has appeared on dozens of magazines and was the first woman featured on the cover of the *FIFA 16* soccer video game. A **star turn** at France 2019 will put her popularity over the top.

MEGAN RAPINOE

With her closely cropped, bleach-blonde hair, winger Megan Rapinoe is impossible to miss when she is on the field. Even without her personal flair, however, Rapinoe would stand out because of her game.

The California native went north to play college soccer at the University of Portland in 2005, leading the Pilots on an undefeated run to the NCAA Division I Championship her freshman year. In the summer before her sophomore year, Rapinoe made her USWNT debut at age twenty-one for Greg Ryan's squad. It was easy to see what Ryan liked about her game. Rapinoe is a creative playmaker and a deft distributor of the ball from the flank. She ranks in the top eight in career assists for the USWNT with more than fifty.

Her scoring totals would be even higher had Rapinoe not had so much injury trouble during her career. She tore the **anterior cruciate ligament (ACL)** in her knee in 2006, 2007, and 2015. These injuries caused her to miss significant time and events such as the 2007 FIFA Women's World Cup and the 2008 Summer Olympic Games in Beijing, China.

Rapinoe was there, however, for the devastating final-match loss to Japan in the 2011 World Cup and for the triumph of winning gold at the 2012 London Olympics. Rapinoe had an excellent tournament in London, scoring three goals, and an excellent year in 2012 overall, scoring eight times and adding twelve assists that season.

The year 2012 was also a big one for Rapinoe personally, because she decided to come out as a lesbian. Since going public about her sexuality, Rapinoe has been an advocate for gay athletes and has been honored by the Los Angeles Gay and Lesbian Center for her support. She was inducted into the National Gay and Lesbian Sports Hall of Fame in 2015.

Of course, that was not the biggest thing that happened to Rapinoe in 2015. She was also part of the USWNT that reclaimed the top spot in the soccer world with a victory at the 2015 FIFA Women's World Cup. Rapinoe scored two goals and set up two others on her team's run to the title. She was a dominant force in the team's opening group-stage match against Australia, scoring twice and claiming Player of the Match honors. Rapinoe was one of five Americans named to the tournament all-star team. If she can remain healthy, Rapinoe is expected to be a playmaking force in France in 2019.

BECKY SAUERBRUNN

Megan Rapinoe holds the FIFA Women's World Cup trophy and waves to fans at the USWNT victory parade in New York City in July 2015.

When Christie Rampone retired in 2015, it was a no-brainer for coach Jill Ellis to name Carli Lloyd as Rampone's replacement as captain. The more surprising move was that Ellis named stalwart defender Becky Sauerbrunn as cocaptain. That simply demonstrates how respected Sauerbrunn is by her teammates and the coaching staff—respect the St. Louis native has earned over more than 130 matches with the USWNT.

Sauerbrunn played her first match for the national team in 2008, after wrapping up a stellar career at the University of Virginia. She started every match of her career with the Cavaliers, but it took some time for Sauerbrunn to find her footing with the USWNT. She did not make the roster for the Olympics in China in 2008. She made the cut for the 2011 FIFA Women's World Cup but played in just one match. Sauerbrunn also made the 2012 Olympic team but played in just three matches in that tournament.

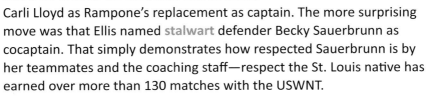

Her breakthrough year finally came in 2013, when Tom Sermanni took over as head coach when Pia Sundhage left the team. Sermanni liked what he saw in the tenacious and steady Sauerbrunn, and she became his regular starter at center back. Sermanni lasted only one season, but it was enough for Sauerbrunn to establish herself to the point that new coach Jill Ellis, who was an assistant under Sundhage, recognized her star potential and allowed her to grow into one of the best defenders in the world.

Sauerbrunn played every second of every U.S. match in the triumphant 2015 FIFA Women's World Cup tournament, and it will be no surprise to see the cocaptain do the same again in 2019.

USWNT cocaptain Becky Sauerbrunn has anchored the defense since 2013.

JULIE JOHNSTON ERTZ

The rise of Arizona's Julie Johnston (she married and changed her name in 2017) may be the most noteworthy development for the current version of the USWNT. Ertz debuted with the national senior team in 2013, her senior year at Santa Clara. At Santa Clara, Ertz starred as a midfielder, but at the national level Sermanni used her as a defender, a role in which she quickly excelled. By the time the 2015 FIFA Women's World Cup came around, Ertz was the starter at center back alongside Sauerbrunn, and that tournament was her coming-out party. The twenty-three-year-old was poised and effective in the USWNT's run to the championship. She and Sauerbrunn never left the field in any U.S. match. Ertz's best showing came against Nigeria in the group stage, a 1–0 U.S. win that secured the group win and earned Ertz Player of the Match honors.

Defender Julie Johnston Ertz has excelled after transitioning from playing the midfield.

Ertz had been fantastic for Ellis and the USWNT, which is what made Ellis's decision to move her to midfield in 2017 so surprising. Ellis is not clairvoyant—Ertz was playing with increasing success at midfield for her club team in Chicago—but she took a chance in breaking up her chemistry with Sauerbrunn. It is a chance that paid off handsomely. Ertz was spectacular for Ellis and her team in 2017, knowing exactly when to attack the box and knowing what to do when she got there.

She scored six goals in 2017, second only to Morgan's seven, and became one of the key players in the lineup through the course of the season. Ertz was so good that she was named U.S. Female Player of the Year for the 2017 season. With Ertz playing alongside Lloyd in the middle, the U.S. midfield will be formidable at France 2019.

SAMANTHA MEWIS

Sam Mewis grew up playing soccer in the suburbs of Boston, MA. In 2011, she travelled far from home to attend UCLA and play for the Bruins. The midfielder helped lead them to the school's very first NCAA Women's Division I Soccer Championship. While at UCLA Mewis played for the national youth teams, but in her junior year she debuted for Ellis' team at the annual Algarve Cup tournament in Portugal. Ellis did not think Mewis (just twenty-two years old at the time) was ready for the 2015 World Cup and left her off the team. Since then, Mewis has made it clear that she is ready for the challenge.

Midfielder Sam Mewis battles a defender for the ball in a match against New Zealand in September 2017.

From the second half of 2015 on, Mewis worked her way not only onto the team, but also into a mainstay in the American midfield. In 2017, Mewis started every USWNT match—a claim only Sauerbrunn could match. Soccer journalist Dan Lauletta described Mewis in glowing terms in a column outlining the top USWNT players in 2017.

"Mewis is the American player who best combines an ability to play the ball on the ground with the size, skill, and desire to be a factor when the ball is in the air. She has the ability to change the point of attack or spring a counterattack with a single touch, even when sitting deep, where she is best able to pull the strings," Lauletta wrote.

At 5 feet 11 inches (1.8 meters), Mewis also possesses the height to give opponents trouble in the air and on set pieces in their end. With the defensively responsible Ertz joining her at midfield in 2017, Mewis has demonstrated a comfort with moving forward and attacking as her high soccer IQ dictates. France 2019 should be a prime opportunity for a star turn from the USWNT's most promising young players.

Other players who will be crucial for the USWNT in France include defenders Kelley O'Hara and Abby Dahlkemper, along with forwards Christen Press and Tobin Heath. All will have to perform well when called upon for the United States to defend its title.

Text-Dependent Questions:

1. How many U.S. Female Player of the Year awards has midfielder Carli Lloyd won?
2. Where did winger Megan Rapinoe play college soccer?
3. How tall is USWNT midfielder Sam Mewis?

Research Project:

Do some research into the Equal Pay for Equal Play campaign supported by many current USWNT players that resulted in a new contract with the United States Soccer Federation in 2017. Outline at least three issues that were in dispute, and compare and contrast what the women were earning compared to their male counterparts. Conclude by discussing whether or not you feel the dispute was resolved fairly.

WORDS TO UNDERSTAND

contingent
a representative group

friendlies
exhibition soccer matches

mantles
positions of people who have responsibility or authority

merit
claim to respect and praise; excellence; worth

CHAPTER 5

The Future of Team USA

The 2016 Olympic Games in Rio de Janeiro, Brazil, were a wake-up call for Ellis and her team. In the women's soccer tournament at those games, Team USA, the three-time defending gold medalists that had never fared worse than the silver medal in any Olympics, finished fifth. Despite the recent World Cup win in 2015, Ellis knew that changes needed to be made for the future. This is why she has given some very young players a long look in preparations for France 2019. She is looking not only at the next World Cup, but also at the next decade for the USWNT.

YOUTH MOVEMENT

In April of 2018, the USWNT played a pair of friendlies against Mexico. At the training camp in preparation for those matches were fourteen players aged twenty-five years old or younger. These ranged from USWNT regulars like midfielder Morgan Brian, who at twenty-five already had more than seventy caps, to nineteen-year-old defender Tierna Davidson, who made her USWNT debut three months earlier. Like Davidson,

Morgan Brian is just one of more than a dozen players twenty-five years of age or younger that coach Jill Ellis auditioned for the USWNT prior to the 2019 FIFA Women's World Cup.

at least twenty new players have come into the fold for the USWNT since the 2016 Olympics, as Ellis expanded the talent pool from autumn 2016 to spring 2018.

STACKED SCHEDULE

These players had plenty of opportunity to make their debuts as Ellis scheduled aggressively in 2017. The team played sixteen matches, the most in a year without a major tournament since 1997. A dozen of those matches came against teams placing fifteen or better in the FIFA world rankings.

"I was willingly and actively looking for the future. Whenever I talk about pressure and this team," Ellis said, "it doesn't matter what everybody else is doing. It's the expectation that's always put on ourselves."

Ellis did not let off the gas to start 2018 either, scheduling eight matches in the first six months. Ellis was constantly evaluating and evolving the team toward a younger group with selections and opportunities earned on merit. That meant some hard choices when it came to players like ninety-eight-match veteran Ali Krieger, the right back for nearly ten years. She will be pushing thirty-five when France 2019 comes around, and there is no indication that Ellis is considering her for the team.

The youth movement on the USWNT following the 2016 Olympics has meant long-time veterans like Ali Krieger, seen here in a match in 2016, are no longer in the picture for the future.

LONG LOOKS

Players like Krieger are not losing their spots to the likes of Emily Sonnett, who is nine years younger than Krieger, because of their birthdates. Neither is Ellis making her decisions on training results and twenty-minute substitution glimpses. Instead, Ellis is giving players long looks, as Dylan Howlett reported in an article for Excelle Sports:

"You can take the approach where you bring in players for ten minutes at the end of each game and they kind of clean up, or you trust them and test them and put them in at the beginning of the game," Ellis said. "That's the approach I took."

PROVING GROUND

One advantage Ellis has had in recent years comes from the rise in popularity of professional women's soccer. In the United States, women's pro soccer comes in the form of the National Women's Soccer League (NWSL), a nine-team league that debuted in 2013. It is the most successful attempt to date at women's pro soccer in North America, because no previous league lasted more than three seasons. The league provides Ellis with a proving ground for players who may not have been on her radar coming out of college but have grown into world-class prospects in roles with their pro teams.

The NWSL is making itself a part of the future of women's soccer in the United States, and pro leagues across the world are following suit. Although the United States is the top nation in women's soccer and the NCAA programs remain the best producers of talent, European women's professional leagues offer more earning potential than playing in college (which has the value of a full four-year scholarship) or the NWSL (the league has a $350,000 per team salary cap). The very best American players have the opportunity to play in Europe.

Meghan Klingenberg, a veteran of more than seventy USWNT matches, plays the ball for the Portland Thorns in a National Women's Soccer League match against the Orlando Pride.

What About the Keeper?

With Hope Solo's departure there is a hole at the goalkeeper position for the first time since 1994, when Briana Scurry made her debut. Head coach Jill Ellis favors Solo's former backup, Alyssa Naeher, as the starter. She will be thirty-two for the 2019 World Cup in France but will have just over thirty caps—not a lot of experience for a goalkeeper at this level.

Naeher's competition appears to be Ashlyn Harris, who is nearly three years older than Naeher but has about half as many caps. Naeher was shaky in goal going into World Cup qualifying, so Ellis may have a difficult decision to make about who is the keeper of the future. For a position that has had so much certainty for so long for Team USA, it may prove to be America's Achilles' heel in defending the World Cup title.

EUROPEAN CLUB SOCCER FOR WOMEN

Barcelona, Paris St. Germain (PSG), Manchester City, Lyon—these are all well-known club teams from Spain, France, and England in men's soccer. In recent years, however, these and other big European clubs have invested significantly in teams for women under their club mantles. These clubs have deep pockets and the ability to outspend the NWSL for talent. USWNT players who left their NWSL teams to play in Europe include: Carli Lloyd, Heather O'Reilly, and Crystal Dunn, who played in England's Women's Super League for City, Arsenal, and Chelsea, respectively, and Morgan, who played at Lyon.

Longtime former USWNT regular Heather O'Reilly (left) battles for the ball in a women's professional match in England.

OBSERVATIONAL OPPORTUNITY

These pro leagues also provide opportunities for Ellis and her staff to watch players in roles other than those in which she is currently using them. It was a move from defense to midfield on her club team in Chicago, for example, that allowed Ellis to see what Ertz brought to the table at that position. Ertz played so well at midfield for Chicago that Ellis could not ignore the results and eventually made the change for her USWNT team as well. It resulted in the best season of Ertz's career at the international level.

STRAIGHT TO PRO

For the top players coming out of high school, big money opportunities overseas are an alternative not only to the NWSL, but to the NCAA as well. This is still rare, but it is possible that the future of the development of the very best U.S. prospects will happen at the professional club level. Two players with the USWNT have recently taken that route, and both are poised to stake a claim to being the future of the USWNT at the 2019 Women's World Cup in France.

LINDSEY HORAN

Horan was a club soccer standout at forward growing up in the Denver area. She quickly gained the attention of the U.S. national program and played for both the under-seventeen and under-twenty teams in high school. Upon graduation, she had a scholarship offer to play at one of the top women's soccer programs in the country at North Carolina, an opportunity any high school player would relish. Horan's talent was such that she had an even better offer, however. French club PSG offered her a six-figure salary to play professional club soccer in Europe, which she did from 2012 to 2016, scoring fifty-four goals in seventy-six matches at forward.

Many USWNT players have taken their skills abroad, either to improve their games or to get a bigger paycheck. From Australia to England and Sweden to France, there is a new world of opportunity out there for top U.S. players.

LINDSEY HORAN

Paris Saint Germain 2012-16

58 MATCHES
46 GOALS

CHRISTEN PRESS

Kopparbergs/Tyresö FF - 2012-2014

47 MATCHES
42 GOALS

MEGHAN KLINGENBERG

Tyresö FF – 2012-14

32 MATCHES
02 GOALS

MEGHAN RAPINOE

Lyon 2013-2014

28 MATCHES
08 GOALS

CASEY SHORT

Avaldsnes IL 2015

27 MATCHES
00 GOALS

AMERICANS ARO

CRYSTAL DUNN

Chelsea 2017-2018

15 MATCHES
03 GOALS

TOBIN HEATH

Paris Saint-Germain 2013-2014

15 MATCHES
04 GOALS

ABBY DAHLKEMPER

Adelaide United-2015-2016

12 MATCHES
05 GOALS

ALLIE LONG

Paris Saint-Germain 2011-12

12 MATCHES
04 GOALS

EMILY SONNET

Sydney FC 2017-2018

12 MATCHES
01 GOALS

UND THE WORLD

Horan's club-level success did not translate to the international level. She debuted for the USWNT in 2013 but played just six matches in three seasons. In 2016, Ellis decided to try Horan as a central midfielder, and she has not looked back. As a midfielder, she has exhibited a consistent ability to distribute the ball to the forwards in just about every circumstance. She knows when to run into space to provide an outlet for her backs and how to fend off defenders to make the right opportunity to go forward, either with a pass or by attacking on her own.

With more than fifty caps under her belt heading into France 2019, she will be just twenty-five years old. Even with a strong midfield **contingent** headed by Mewis, Ertz, and Lloyd, Horan could be the breakout player of the event for the USWNT.

MALLORY PUGH

Midfielder Lindsey Horan will be one of the USWNT's young stars to watch in France in 2019.

That is, unless forward Mallory Pugh steals the breakout spotlight. Pugh will be only twenty-one in France, but with more than thirty-five caps the youngster has already earned the trust of Ellis.

Like Horan, Pugh is part of the future of Team USA, and she turned down a college scholarship to turn pro instead. Pugh, also from the Denver area, was slated to play at UCLA. Ultimately, she chose instead to play with the Washington Spirit of the NWSL, debuting for the club in 2017. As a member of the USWNT since 2013 the national team pays her NWSL salary, which does not count against the salary cap.

Even as a teenager, Pugh was flat-out dangerous. Despite rarely playing a full match and playing mostly as a substitute, Pugh scored in about every third appearance. In two back-to-back wins over Mexico in April of 2018, Pugh and Rapinoe worked well together when Pugh subbed in during the second half of each match. The veteran set up the young player for goals in each match.

Ellis trusts Pugh in big games as well. As an eighteen-year-old, Pugh not only made the eighteen-player Olympic roster for the games in Brazil but also played in three matches. She scored after subbing in for Rapinoe in a group-stage match against Colombia. There is ample evidence that Pugh is a special player, and many people suggest she will benefit from taking a special path.

Mallory Pugh was just seventeen years old when she debuted for the USWNT in 2013.

Sports Illustrated *spotlights the USWNT's Mallory Pugh for its Rising Stars series.*

WAVE OF THE FUTURE

For most players, few will argue that going the college route is the best step for their development. More than a few, however, have started to express that this might not be true for the top players.

Former USWNT two-time Player of the Year and former head coach April Heinrichs is among those who believes going pro can be the right move. Heinrichs, now the technical director for U.S. Women's Soccer, has praised the way the European clubs set up their development systems. In Europe, the top clubs all run youth training academies, so the best prospects are immersed in professional training environments as young teenagers.

Standout Canadian player Kadeisha Buchanan chose to develop her game at the University of West Virginia before turning pro.

Heinrichs's opinion is echoed by John Herdman, the head coach of the Canadian men's national team. Male and female players from Canada have also traditionally chosen to play on scholarship at American universities to develop their skills. For example, superstar forward Christine Sinclair played at the University of Portland. More recently, star defender Kadeisha Buchanan graduated from the University of West Virginia in 2016 before signing to play for Lyon in France. Herdman, who grew up in England, is a proponent of players being exposed to professional training environments as well.

For male stars, skipping college to play professionally in Europe has been an option for decades, and more recently this is becoming the case in Major League Soccer. For women the opportunities are brand-new, with the ability to play pro at home included from the beginning.

Though this development model may be the wave of the future in women's soccer, it is just a ripple in the pond today. More women will surely follow in the footsteps of Pugh and Horan as the United States continues to produce some of the best players in the world. Those opportunities will continue to be limited to the best of the best, however, until the women's sport can grow to the point that it can generate fan interest, and therefore revenue, in significant amounts year-round, rather than just every four summers.

Text-Dependent Questions:

1. How old was Morgan Brian when she played her seventieth match for the USWNT?

2. Where did Lindsey Horan grow up?

3. How old was Mallory Pugh when she was selected for the United States Olympic team in 2016?

Research Project:

Name your own twenty-three woman USWNT roster for the 2019 World Cup with a sentence or two that supports each selection. Then name your starting eleven, and explain your reasoning.

Club: collective name for a team, and the organization that runs it.

CONCACAF: acronym for the *Confederation of North, Central American and Caribbean Association Football*, the governing body of the sport in North and Central America and the Caribbean; pronounced "kon-ka-kaff".

Extra time: additional period, normally two halves of 15 minutes, used to determine the winner in some tied cup matches.

Full-time: the end of the game, signaled by the referees whistle (also known as the *final whistle*).

Goal difference: net difference between goals scored and goals conceded. Used to differentiate league or group stage positions when clubs are tied on points.

Hat trick: when a player scores three goals in a single match.

Own goal: where a player scores a goal against her own team, usually as the result of an error.

Penalty area: rectangular area measuring 44 yards (40.2 meters) by 18 yards (16.5 meters) in front of each goal; commonly called "the box".

Penalty kick: kick taken 12 yards (11 meters) from goal, awarded when a team commits a foul inside its own penalty area.

Penalty shootout: method of deciding a match in a knockout competition, which has ended in a draw after full-time and extra-time. Players from each side take turns to attempt to score a penalty kick against the opposition goalkeeper. Sudden death is introduced if scores are level after each side has taken five penalties.

Side: Another word for team

Stoppage time: an additional number of minutes at the end of each half, determined by the match officials, to compensate for time lost during the game. Informally known by various names, including *injury time* and *added time*.

UEFA: acronym for *Union of European Football Associations*, the governing body of the sport in Europe; pronounced "you-eh-fa".

Davis, Noah, and Leddy, Rick. *Road to Glory: The U.S. Women's Soccer Team,* Beverley Hills, CA: Sole Books, 2015.

Jökulsson, Illugi. *U.S. Women's Team: Soccer Champions.* New York, NY: Abbeville Press, 2015.

Nash, Tim. *It's Not the Glory: The Remarkable First Thirty Years of U.S. Women's Soccer.* Morrisville, NC: Lulu Publishing, 2016.

Savage, Jeff. U.S. *Women's National Team: Soccer Champions* Minneapolis, MN: Lerner Books, 2018.

Seigerman, David. *Becky Sauerbrunn.* New York, NY: Aladdin Press, 2017.

INTERNET RESOURCES

https://sbisoccer.com/ An internet news site focused on the coverage of American and international soccer

https://www.fourfourtwo.com/us The website of the UK's favorite monthly soccer publication

https://www.ussoccer.com/ The official site of the governing body of soccer in the United States

https://www.si.com/planet-futbol Soccer coverage from the website of *Sports Illustrated*, a weekly sports publication

https://www.starsandstripesfc.com/ American soccer coverage from SBNation, a site comprising 320 blogs covering individual professional and college sports teams, and other sports-oriented topics.

INDEX

AUTHOR'S BIOGRAPHY

Andrew Luke is a former journalist, reporting on both sports and general news for many years at television stations in various locations across the United States affiliated with NBC, CBS and Fox. Prior to his journalism career he worked with the Boston Red Sox Major League baseball team. An avid writer and sports enthusiast, he has authored over thirty books on sports topics. In his downtime Andrew enjoys family time with his wife and two young children and attending hockey, football, and baseball games.

EDUCATIONAL VIDEO LINKS

Chapter 1: http://x-qr.net/1Gxs
Chapter 2: http://x-qr.net/1D94
Chapter 3: http://x-qr.net/1E8x

Chapter 4: http://x-qr.net/1GmN
Chapter 5: http://x-qr.net/1GfT

PICTURE CREDITS